IF FAILURE WAS A PERSON

From Chicago to Seattle, from Failing to Rising

Anthony Curtis

Contents

ANTHONY CURTIS

ISBN: 979-8-234-05101-1 (Paperback)

Federal Way, Washington
First Edition, 2026

If Failure Was a Person

If failure was a person, they'd be misunderstood.

They wouldn't wear fancy clothes or drive the cleanest car. They'd sometimes show up late, tired but still present. Every room they'd walk into would get quiet, because people would rather celebrate success than sit next to the one who had taught them it.

Failure is that real friend, the one who doesn't flatter you, doesn't sugarcoat, and doesn't pretend. It's the friend who'll tell you straight up, "You weren't ready yet." It's the one who humbles you enough to grow and toughens you enough to last.

Failure will expose what wasn't built to endure. It'll show you who claps for you when you win and who disappears when you fall. It'll strip away your pride, the ego, and the illusion of control. But what failure leaves behind is purpose. What it leaves behind is you: raw, refined, and ready.

Because here's the truth. Every success story you've admired has a failure somewhere in its credits. The difference is that some people hide theirs, while others use theirs to build something greater.

Some things about failure you will want to keep in mind:

1. Failure doesn't mean you're unqualified. It means you're still learning.
2. Every stumble prepares you for the weight of what's coming next.

3. Failure removes what doesn't belong. Sometimes what you lose is what you were never meant to carry with you into your next season.
4. Failure humbles you before success can expose you. If you can't handle minor disappointments privately, big victories will crush you publicly.
5. Failure introduces you to faith. It's easy to believe when everything is going right. But when everything falls apart and you still move forward? That is real faith.

My Principles

1. **Strong Decisions and Discipline.** Embrace the art of self-discipline and make strong decisions without compromising your values.
2. **Value-Based Decision Making.** Learn the mantra, "If it doesn't evolve you, it doesn't involve you."
3. **Value Focus.** Master the principle of "minding the business that pays you."
4. **Proactive Health and Wealth.** Take a proactive approach to your health and wealth by understanding their critical role in your life.
5. **Self-Control and Consistency.** Develop self-control and understand the importance of staying consistent in your efforts.

Outcome

These are not just ideas; they are outcomes. If you apply these principles daily, you will develop a resilient, focused mindset equipped to navigate life's challenges and build sustained success.

I didn't just create these principles in comfort. I forged them through loss, failure, discipline, and maturity. As I grew older, after my cousins were killed in Chicago, after my father and grandfather passed, and as time became shorter and more precious, I realized I couldn't keep drifting through life reacting to everything around me.

I had to become laser-focused. Focused on my goals. Focused on my dreams. And focused on building something bigger than my past. I learned to keep my eyes on the prize and off other people's plates. Comparison drains purpose. Energy is currency. And as my mentor and coach E.T. says, "Where your focus goes, your energy flows."

I figured out something simple but powerful: I didn't have to be the smartest in the room. I just had to get there earlier, stay a little longer, and remain consistent. These principles came from self-education, repeated failures, and intentional growth. They became my internal code; not just for survival, but for evolution.

If you apply them daily, they can become yours too.

Introduction

The Label of Failure

In a world quick to label, being called a "failure" is one of the harshest tags a person can carry. It's a word that doesn't just describe; it seems to dictate.

Being labeled a failure doesn't just hurt your feelings; it shapes how you see yourself and how you move through the world. It affects how you show up in rooms where you feel inferior, how you speak when opportunity presents itself, and whether you even believe you deserve certain jobs, relationships, or spaces. When you internalize that label, you begin to self-sabotage before anyone else gets the chance. You settle for less. You align with people who reinforce that identity. And over time, you lose the ability to assess your strengths honestly because you've already convinced yourself you don't have any. That label becomes a ceiling you never try to break through.

But what if failure was not just a word, but a person? What if that person were me, or even you?

My story isn't just about the challenges and setbacks I faced growing up on the South Side of Chicago and later in Seattle. It's about the journey of a young person constantly battling the label of "failure," a label my father, society, and at times, even the mirror staring back at me gave me.

What if I told you that failure could become one of your greatest teachers in life? What are some of the areas where others have labeled you a failure? Take this time to reflect on your biggest struggle and write down two things you can actually learn from it.

Chapter One

The F Bomb

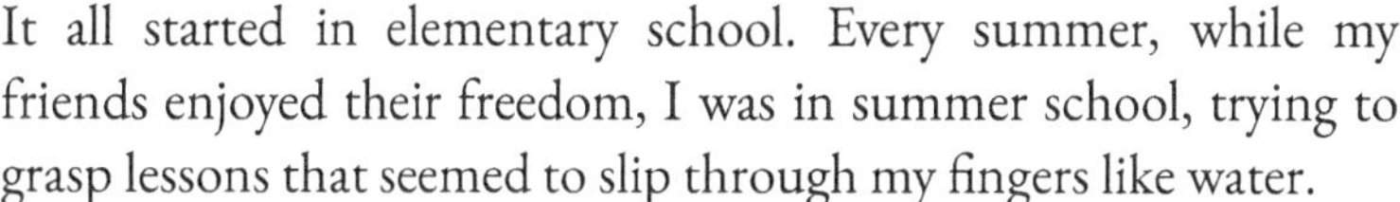

It all started in elementary school. Every summer, while my friends enjoyed their freedom, I was in summer school, trying to grasp lessons that seemed to slip through my fingers like water.

Trauma and dysfunction filled my childhood. Every day, going to school was some kind of struggle or battle. Either something was happening at home with my parents; in the community with violence, police, gangs, and drugs; or even worse, at school.

I never fully understood how dangerous it was just to get to school and back until later in life. At any moment, a shootout could break out between rival gangs. That wasn't something we saw on the news; it was normal life. I remember one school night, a robbery took place next door. The police usually came a little after the crime for different reasons. The next morning, we still had to get up, get dressed, and pretend everything was normal.

Another time, I had just gotten home. I was settling in, probably thinking about what we were going to eat or where I was going to go that evening, when gunshots rang out. A drive-by happened right outside our house. You learn to drop to the floor before you even think. That's not fear: that's conditioning.

On 104th and Wabash, we would often start trouble with the older guys on our block. We were young, reckless, and trying to prove something. One day it went too far. What started as playing escalated into violence, and my brother ended up with a broken collarbone. That's how thin the line was between "fun" and trauma where we grew up.

I could tell a hundred stories like that. More stories than I have pages. But the point is this: when chaos becomes your normal, survival becomes your mindset.

Pirie, Khon, Swift, and Gillespie were the grammar schools I attended in Chicago, and I always had to walk to and from school. That meant I was fighting, helping someone else fight, or running from some kind of trouble. On top of that, I struggled with a learning disability I didn't yet understand, in a system that didn't know how to, or care to, understand me. School wasn't a place of safety or curiosity. It was survival. Every year was a challenge, a test I was never taught to prepare for, and I did just enough to get by.

But if I'm being real, grammar school didn't just challenge me; it **shaped how I view education to this day**. It failed me early. Repeatedly. Systemically.

My experience within the system shaped my relationship with education. Most of the schools I attended were in predominantly Black, underserved neighborhoods where resources often felt limited and classrooms were overcrowded. From a student's perspective, it didn't feel like there was space for individual attention, especially for students struggling quietly.

Teachers often had to implement a one-size-fits-all model. The curriculum moved at a fixed pace, regardless of whether students could keep up or they fell behind. If you didn't grasp the material the first way a teacher explained it, there wasn't always time to approach it differently. Students who learned at different speeds or processed information differently received labels quickly, sometimes as distractions or problems, and often became candidates for special education or summer school.

I don't say this to criticize teachers. Many of them likely did best they could within the system. But from where I stood as a student, the system rarely accounted for different learning styles, trauma backgrounds, or environmental pressures. When your nervous system is constantly on alert outside school, it's hard to sit still and absorb algebra inside it.

Over time, I internalized the idea that if I wasn't succeeding in that structure, then I must not be built for success. It took years for me to realize that intelligence and potential don't always show up the way standardized education expects them to.

Today, my work with youth is rooted in helping to create the support system I wish I had.

Kohn Elementary hit me the hardest. When I walked through the front doors, I passed through metal detectors. Immediately to my left was a table, laid out like inventory, with knives, BB guns, tasers, and other weapons confiscated from students. That was normal. That was routine. And that was my life for third and fourth grade.

Kohn is also where teachers and curriculum labeled me; where my diagnosis, more than my potential, shaped my academic identity. Special education. Learning disability. Boxes I didn't ask to be placed in, but ones I carried with me long after I left that building.

Math was like an uncrackable code to me. On every report card, amid a sea of grades that rarely rose above a *D*, one constant remained: that solid *F* in math. It was not just a letter. It was a reminder, an echo in the halls of my mind that repeated the same word: failure.

My father, determined to fix this, would have me sit at the kitchen table for hours counting money. It should have been a simple task, but the numbers danced before my eyes in a confusing jumble. His patience would wear thin, and disappointment turned into frustration, both his and mine. His frustration would often turn physical, with him throwing his keys at me, threatening to give me a roundhouse kick, or me getting a belt to the a**.

Those long evenings became more than lessons in arithmetic, more than just counting money. They were lessons in fear and identity. They counted worth, mine. And most days, I came up short. Every mistake felt like proof that something was wrong with me, not with the work. I didn't just struggle with math. I wrestled with the belief that I might actually be broken in a way that I couldn't fix. Shame crept in quietly and sat beside me. It whispered that maybe that was who I really was: slow, behind, and less than.

The word "failure" didn't always come out of my father's mouth. My report cards proved that every semester. The red ink on my papers did that. The *F*s stacked up, marking me repeatedly.

But at home, those grades had consequences.

My punishments were tied to those *F*s. And while my father may not have said, "You are a failure," in those exact words, he used words like "stupid," "dumb," and "idiot."

Over time, the message became clear. When your grades are failing and your character is being attacked at the same time, it doesn't take much for a child to connect the dots.

The school labeled my performance.

Home reinforced the identity.

And eventually, I stopped separating the two.

That was when my failure identity took root. It did not arrive loudly. It slipped in silently and wrapped itself around my confidence. I believed that failure was not just something that happened to me. It was what I was. It seeped beyond school, into how I saw myself, and shaped the way I walked into rooms, how I tried, and too often, how I stopped trying. Fear told me not to mess up. Shame told me I already had. Yet somewhere, buried beneath all that weight, my resilience refused to die. Even when I felt defeated, something in me kept showing up to that table, even if it meant sitting there with trembling hands and tired eyes.

But in ways I could not see then, God was strengthening me in those moments. Every tear, every sigh, every quiet repeated try built muscle I did not know I would need later. Those moments prepared me, even while I felt like they were crushing me.

Those were the early days of a journey, one that became as much about unlearning labels as it did about learning everything else. Every *F* was not a full stop. It was a comma, a pause before the next chapter of my story. Still, the repetitive cycle of counting and failing took a toll. That toll went beyond mental exhaustion. It marked the beginning of a trauma that lingered, and that feeling of dread became a constant companion, stretching its shadow across other parts of my life.

The term PTSD is often associated with soldiers and catastrophic events. Yet there I was, a child sitting at a kitchen table, experiencing my own battlefield of numbers. The scars were not visible, but they were deep, and they shaped how I saw myself and the world around me.

On top of my learning disability, Kohn was on probation. That meant we couldn't leave campus, ever, because the school was too dangerous, too chaotic, too destructive. Kids acted out trauma they didn't have language for, and adults tried to manage it without the tools, support, or cultural understanding needed to do it right.

Most of the teachers were white or came from suburban backgrounds and commuted into an inner-city, predominantly Black and brown school. There was a massive cultural disconnect. What they saw as "defiance," we lived as survival. What they called "disruption" was often unaddressed pain.

That disconnect didn't just hurt students; it put teachers at risk too.

I remember a white teacher getting attacked when he walked to his car after school. The violence was so serious that he had to be hospitalized. That moment burned into my memory, not just because it was tragic, but because it showed how broken the system was on every level. Nobody was winning. Not students. Not teachers. And definitely not the community.

The school went up to eighth grade, and the student who attacked him was older; a year or two ahead of me at the time. I was about eight years old. I don't remember every detail clearly, but I remember the feeling.

After that day, the entire school shifted. Teachers moved differently. Adults were tense. Students whispered. You could feel that something serious had happened.

For an eight-year-old, seeing violence come from someone just a little older than you changes how you see school. It stops feeling like a safe place for learning and starts feeling unpredictable.

That day was traumatic, not just for me, but for the entire community.

And that's just one school.

I have more stories like that, too many to fit on these pages. Horror stories. Quiet ones. Loud ones. Moments that shaped how I saw authority, safety, learning, and myself. Grammar school wasn't a foundation; it was a battlefield. And I carried those lessons with me far longer than any report card.

That was where I formed my relationship with school.

It didn't form by inspiration, but by experience. Not by possibility, but by containment.

And yet... I'm still here.

One year, while attending Kohn, an accident resulted in me losing the tip of my finger.

The impact was immediate. There wasn't time to react. One second, I casually leaned against a door; the next there was a sharp, overwhelming pain. Everything blurred together: the door slamming, my body jolting forward, and the shock before the pain fully registered.

It wasn't intentional. And it wasn't a fight. But it was another reminder of how unpredictable my environment felt. Even on what seemed like a normal day, things could shift in a second.

I will talk more in depth about the emotional aftermath of that day later, as the physical pain healed much faster than the internal impact did.

That same year, I faced the very real possibility of repeating the third or fourth grade because academically I was still struggling. I wasn't passing tests. I wasn't grasping the curriculum.

After the door incident, the school installed slow-close mechanisms to prevent it from happening again. My family didn't pursue legal action, so no public escalation.

Looking back, I've often wondered if that played a role in what happened next.

Despite failing academically, the school allowed me to move up to the next grade. There was no grand explanation. No ceremony. Just a quiet advancement, perhaps in silent acknowledgment of my battle fought behind the scenes. It was another year of falling short on paper.

At the time, I didn't question it. I just moved forward.

It was much harder to pass classes back in the mid-90s than today; you had to really put in the work, or you didn't advance to the next grade. Period!

But as an adult, I can't help but reflect on how systems sometimes operate quietly behind the scenes, and how some people make certain decisions without ever speaking out loud.

Moments like those did more than just mark my childhood. They shaped how I saw myself, how I carried pain, and how I started believing certain things about who I was.

Go Deeper: Education and Being Labeled a Failure

Scan this QR code to hear me speak directly about what it felt like being labeled a failure in school and how that label shaped me before I learned how to reshape it.

Reflection Questions

- When did you first start believing something negative about yourself?

....

....

....

....

....

- Whose voice shaped your view of yourself, and does their voice deserve that much power?

....
....
....
....
....

- What might happen if you stopped calling yourself a "failure" and instead called yourself a "work in progress"?

....
....
....
....
....

Chapter Two

I Moved; Failure Didn't

We moved to Seattle in 2001, the year I entered seventh grade. The city promised a fresh start. New schools, fresh faces, yet the same old label followed me. But what does a fresh start really mean for a young soul already shaped by struggle and survival? A new city does not erase old scars. It simply gives them a new place to ache.

My mother didn't just wake up one day and decide to move us across the country. Before Seattle, there were years of running. We moved all over Chicago: the North Side, different parts of the South Side, and stayed with relatives and family friends. That's when I attended Gillespie and Swift. We weren't moving for opportunity. We were moving for safety.

My father was abusive and unfaithful. I won't pretend my mother was perfect, but she tried to survive. She wanted to protect us. Every move was an attempt to increase the distance from him.

Eventually, she realized she couldn't fully escape him while we were still in Chicago. Around that time, she reconnected with my future stepfather, the father of three of my siblings. He was traveling back and forth between Chicago and Seattle. When the opportunity arose, my mother followed him to the Pacific Northwest.

That's how we landed in Seattle.

This chapter of my life was not just about a physical move from one city to another. It was about the internal migration of a young soul searching for identity in unfamiliar territory. Seattle was supposed to be a new beginning, but for me, it became a continuation of a battle I had fought all my life: the battle to discover who I was beyond the labels and survival tactics.

People told me I had an accent. The slang and basic terminology on the West Coast were completely different from those in the Midwest. I had to explain almost every word that came out of my mouth. It honestly felt like I was on a completely different planet.

What no one sees in a move like that is the emotional confusion it stirs. A part of me wanted to believe Seattle might be different, that maybe I could breathe and not feel hunted by life. But another part of me refused to relax. I didn't know how to live without survival mode. I only knew how to stay ready. So even in a new place, I moved cautiously, watching and reading every room to figure out where I fit, or if I even fit at all. I was physically in a new city, but mentally I was still in Chicago, bracing for the world to hit me first.

Chicago had taught me the language of the streets: how to fight, rob, and survive. Those lessons had etched themselves deep, embedded into my instincts and identity. I had learned to keep my guard up, never show weakness, and move as if life always waited for me to slip. Seattle, with its different rhythm and unfamiliar environment, presented a new battlefield. I carried more than just physical baggage. I carried a mindset forged in the Wild 100s and the South Side of Chicago, a mindset that believed survival was my first job and trust was a luxury I could not afford.

My early days in Seattle were a mix of curiosity and cautious navigation. Seattle felt different, quieter in some ways. Yet beneath the surface, there were familiar patterns. I quickly realized that survival skills, once learned, do not disappear. They adapt.

Seattle's streets had their own codes, dangers, and opportunities. I learned new lessons. Some were harsh. Some were misguided. All of them became threads in the tapestry of my journey. The streets spoke a language I understood; they offered a different education. It was there that I sharpened my instincts for survival and rebellion.

Crime, though never a righteous path, did not feel like a choice. It felt like a necessity, a path shaped by circumstance and a response to a world that seemed to have no place for me. My siblings and I lived in survival mode. Stealing cars for joyrides was not just about the adrenaline rush. It became a misguided expression of freedom and control in a life where I felt powerless. Each stolen moment of freedom behind the wheel stood in stark contrast to the confinement I felt in every other area of my life.

I'm one of six children: one older brother, two older sisters, one younger sister, and one younger brother. Our family dynamic had layers we didn't fully understand at the time. Some of us didn't even realize we had different fathers until later in life. That truth unfolded slowly, piece by piece, as we grew older.

We moved from house to house, stole what we needed, and took advantage of good people who helped us more than our own parents. Stealing wasn't just an act of rebellion. It was a survival tactic; a skill honed through necessity and desperation. We lived in the moment with little regard for tomorrow.

And that is when I learned this truth. Survival skills do not disappear. They adapt. The real challenge is learning how to transform survival into purpose and pain into direction.

Constant change and the deepening of old habits marked my middle school years. Those years were less about textbooks and classrooms and more about life lessons learned outside them. I lived a dual life: a student by day, barely engaged, and a street-savvy survivor by night. Like in Chicago, I moved middle schools often, from Meany Middle School to Madrona, and then to Triple A (African American Academy).

Amid this chaos, I carved out an identity for myself. It was a rough draft, written in the language of the streets. "Create yourself an image," I told myself. "Use what you have to manipulate and control." That became my survival mantra, a code that seemed to make sense in a world that often didn't.

But it wasn't all about survival. There was an unspoken understanding among those of us living on the edge. "Don't make enemies unless you absolutely have to." It wasn't only about physical confrontation. It was about choosing your battles, knowing when to stand your ground, when to walk away, and when to build bridges you may need to cross later. I found out later in life that was a gift I naturally possessed.

The thing I eventually discovered about myself, something school never measured, was my gift for building relationships. I've always been a people person. Even in the middle of chaos, I could connect. I can read a room. I can feel the energy. And I can build trust quickly.

What I didn't understand back then was that this gift could build something powerful or fuel something destructive. The same relationship skills I once used to survive in the streets are the same skills I use to mentor, speak, and build community.

That realization gave me hope. It taught me that just because your environment shapes you, it doesn't mean it gets the final say. Sometimes the very traits that got you through the storm are the ones that will help you build something better on the other side.

Those middle school years were not just a footnote in my academic record. They were a critical phase in my life story; years filled with contradiction and conflict, marked by the slow and often painful forging of identity. They laid the foundation for who I would become, for better or worse. Moving to a new place did not erase what was happening inside me. It only revealed how much I still wrestled with who I was, what I carried, and what I was becoming.

Reflection Questions

- Have you ever moved, switched schools, gotten new friends, or changed environments and still felt the same inside?

....
....
....
....
....

- What habits or mindsets followed you into your "new beginning"?

....
....
....
....
....

- What survival skill are you still using that helped you once but is hurting you now?

....
....
....
....
....

Chapter Three

Nothing Beats a Failure but a Try

Middle school had almost wrapped up, and things were getting better for me. Maybe it was because I didn't have parents who constantly watched over me. My mom hustled hard to keep us afloat and get ready to welcome my little brother into the world. She even did ten days in jail while pregnant for selling drugs. Meanwhile, my stepdad was in and out; sometimes he disappeared for days or weeks, caught up in his own struggles with drugs or landing back in jail.

Seventh grade was when I landed at Meany and Madrona in the Central District. New city, new school, new rules. I felt isolated more than anything else. I met a few solid people, but I still felt out of place. Culture shock is the only way I can describe it.

Switching schools that often does something to you. It disrupts your rhythm and messes with your confidence. It forces you to re-adapt before you can ever get comfortable. And when you're already carrying trauma and a learning disability, that instability hits differently.

Academically, though, I'll say this: school in Seattle felt easier than in Chicago. Violence inside the building wasn't as normalized. Teachers seemed more patient. There was more structure. Inner city Seattle versus inner city Chicago was night and day.

But just because it felt easier didn't mean I felt secure.

I still worried about being held back. I still compared myself to my siblings, who adapted academically better than I did. That comparison sat heavily. I wasn't failing at the same rate as before, but I wasn't excelling either. I was floating in the middle, unnoticed, uncertain, and trying not to sink.

Looking back, I realize something else. In the mid-90s and early 2000s, there weren't as many visible community-based organizations, mentors, or youth leaders as there are today. I don't remember anyone breaking down the history of education, discipline policies, or the school-to-prison pipeline. I didn't understand the system; I experienced it.

And that difference matters.

But here's the game changer: my eighth-grade math teacher at Triple A. That dude was different. He'd look me straight in the eye, as if he stared into my soul, and tell me straight up, "I'm not letting you fail." That hit differently. No other Black man, no man at all for that matter, had ever said anything like that to me. And he meant it. I barely made it, but I graduated from eighth grade. It was a close call, but I did it.

By that time, I was pretty much on my own. Things were a little more stable, though. We'd come a long way from sleeping in cars, crashing with strangers and addicts, and staying in drug-infested motels. We moved into Seattle emergency housing on 12th and Fir, right across from Yesler Terrace. After that, we landed at the YWCA down the street from the Garfield Community Center in the Central District. It was an all-women and children's shelter. My mom and sisters would sneak my stepdad, my brother, and me in after hours so we could have a place to sleep.

By thirteen or fourteen, I knew the score. Mom couldn't support me financially anymore, so I had to hustle to feed myself and keep up appearances. I had to look like I had money, even when I didn't. It was about survival, but it was also about pride and making sure I didn't stand out for the wrong reasons.

My idea of making money was whatever I could get away with. Shooting dice. Stealing from stores. Taking things from people when I thought I wouldn't get caught. If it brought in cash or was something I could flip, I was in. But it wasn't all illegal. I raked leaves. Did little side jobs. Helped clean up. Whatever someone would pay me for. The problem was I didn't want slow money. I wanted quick money. I wanted to feel something in my pocket.

And if I'm being real, I leaned on people too. I'd let girls buy things for me. I'd take advantage of situations if it benefited me. At that age, I wasn't thinking long term. I was just thinking about what made me feel good in the moment.

High school felt like stepping into a different world, one where survival took on new meanings. Freshman year, I found my tribe, a group of kids who understood my life because it was theirs too. Single parents, or no parents; all of us struggled with identity, respect, and just getting through each day. We weren't just friends; we were allies in a battle we knew too well. We all went to Rainier Beach High School, and many of us lived in the Ville across the street. That meant we could go home to each other's houses for lunch, or steal food from Rite Aid/QFC. Sometimes we'd even sneak off campus during lunch to lift the latest drip from Southcenter Mall.

Meeting Antoine was a game-changer. He was the first person in Washington I could truly call a best friend. With him, I started exploring a new idea. What if I could disguise my failures? What if I could wear a mask that showed the world a different version of me? It wasn't just about survival anymore. It was about acceptance and finding a place in a world that constantly pushed me to the sidelines.

In the hallways and classrooms, I played my role. I did just enough work to scrape by, nodded along in class, and put on a front that said, "I get it." It was a balancing act to pretend to belong to a system I felt disconnected from. But it worked, in its own way. I moved from grade to grade, each step a quiet victory in a personal war.

Despite my efforts, I knew where I stood. I wasn't the guy with the looks or the brains. I had crooked teeth, a head that didn't quite grasp numbers or words, and no money in my pocket. That was my reality. But I had something else. Maybe it was charm. People seemed to enjoy having me around, and in the high school hierarchy, that counted for something.

Then there was my older brother, Daniel, over at Renton High School; a sharp contrast to my own high school persona. From the very beginning, we were glued at the hip. He was my built-in protector. Wherever he went, I was close behind. For most of our childhood, he carried that responsibility. He kept me close, kept me safe as best he could. He's my right hand. Always has been. And still is to this day. He was the guy everyone knew: smart, athletic, the basketball player with a bright future. He adapted quickly and built an image that people admired. When he left home, he was determined to return as a completely different person and change his financial and social status. And he succeeded by any means necessary. And me? I felt like I lived in his shadow and had to search for my own spotlight. I wasn't the sports guy or the academic ace. My skills were fast-talking rhymes and cracking jokes. That became my ticket to recognition, my way of saying, "Hey, I'm here too."

High school was a mix of pretending and discovering, of hiding some truths while revealing others. It was about learning the art of survival in a social jungle, where every step could mean a rise or a fall. It was there, in those bustling halls and crowded classrooms, that I pieced together who I thought I was and who I wanted to become.

After my ninth-grade year at Rainier Beach High School, I spent the summer back in Chicago. It was my first visit to Chicago since moving to Seattle, and my father was already caring for another family. Back then, I knew better than to ask many questions; if I did, he'd either lie to me or I'd get into serious trouble. All I knew was that he had given up on us, and I had to adapt. However, for the first time, I felt like my father was a little proud of me, simply because I had made it through my freshman year without failing or having to attend summer school. All my siblings were naturally strong in formal education. It just didn't interest me, sadly enough.

I wrapped up my summer in Chicago and headed back to Seattle, stepping into a brand new year in unfamiliar territory after being homeless, broke, and labeled a failure. I returned with a whole new drive and passion for life. And even though that might sound positive or inspiring, I had no intention of becoming a better person. I wanted to be a baller, a street legend, a hood N****a, well respected and praised by the world.

Back then, I wore a chip on my shoulder and my heart on my sleeve. In other words, I had one thing to prove. If the world saw me as a failure, I fully accepted that label. And I was determined to be the greatest failure humanity had ever known.

Fasten your seatbelts and let me take you on a ride through the mind of teenage Anthony, also known as PAPA.

Chapter Four

Fail Big or Stay Small

"Papa" wasn't a name I earned on the streets. It was a name I received at birth. My mama told me when I came out, I had hair around the sides of my head and was bald in the middle. I looked like a little old man. So immediately they started calling me Papa. That was it. But somewhere along the way, I flipped it; I turned it into something else. I wanted the world to believe Papa was an OG name. I made the girls think it meant "big man on campus," and let people assume it stood for power.

Truth is, it stood for confusion. I was in a full-blown identity crisis.

I moved to 216th and Pacific Highway right after my summer in Chicago and enrolled at Mount Rainier. We landed at the Marina Club Apartments, which they now call Majestic Bay. For me, it might as well have been another planet. I had to make new friends, start over at a new high school, and learn how to move, grind, and hustle in territory I didn't understand. It was culture shock all over again.

I wasn't downtown, and I wasn't in the Central District or the South End. I was in the Highway, and it had its own rhythm, its own codes; a mix of characters, chaos, and unspoken rules.

It didn't take long for me to find my people, Sam and Kev, better known as Turt and Worm. From day one, we moved like brothers. Same mindset. Same hunger. We figured out the school and the streets together.

We skipped class to shoot dice, fought for no reason other than ego, dug in purses when backs were turned, and swiped wallets during weight training. There were bank scams, robberies, and we sold weed and crack in and out of school. We flipped clothes, traded gear, and bought jewelry. Whatever hustle showed up, we ran with it. The grind wasn't just about money; it was about momentum. About feeling like we mattered in a world that never made space for us. In other words, we lived recklessly but moved sneakily.

Mount Rainier was also where everything shifted for me. It's where I began discovering my gift. And it's where I learned my first real lessons about relationships, loyalty, and failure.

My tenth-grade year felt like a movie with no script and no safety net. During that school year, I was in a total of four relationships. Only four, but they taught me everything I thought I knew, and everything I didn't. I genuinely tried to be faithful and got played. Something in me snapped. But how do you have successful relationships if you've never seen one done right? When dysfunction is your blueprint, how are you supposed to build something healthy?

My uncle used to pull up to Chicago with a new woman almost every time while still married. My parents had one of the most toxic relationships I've ever witnessed. One of my grandmas has been single for as long as I can remember. Still is. But she's happy, and that's what matters. My other grandma? Maybe she thought she was in a monogamous relationship. Maybe she didn't. Either way, she looked happy. And at that age, I didn't feel like it was my place to question it.

In tenth grade, I ran through every emotion: anger, betrayal, confusion, numbness. After suffering heartbreak, I hardened my heart and made a promise to myself that every girl after that would pay for what I went through, but I'll get into that more at another time. I started watching player movies. I surrounded myself with guys who didn't show actual emotion, didn't show sympathy, and didn't show vulnerability. They treated girls like disposable objects. Like recycle bins.

And I followed that model. Not because I was heartless, but because I was hurt. Where I came from, being in pain and showing emotion as a Black boy wasn't just seen as weakness; it made you prey. And there were sharks everywhere. So I asked myself a question: Do I want to be a shark, or shark bait? By any means necessary, that decision felt easy. I built a monster.

There's not enough time to explain every moment, but just know this: I was spiraling. In my head, I wasn't just trying to survive anymore. I was trying to be the next big thing; I was chasing extremes. I was trying to fail bigger than anyone else.

Real talk, I was a product of my environment. And when you live recklessly, numb, and disconnected, life has a way of reminding you how fragile you really are.

When I was sixteen, I had my first near-death experience in Seattle. I was jumped by more than ten people.

It wasn't exactly personal, but it wasn't completely random either. We knew of each other. Same circles. Same environment. But that night, between it being dark and the other group being high and drunk, they were looking for trouble. And if I'm being honest, so was I.

Nobody had a real reason. No deep history. Just pride, energy, and the need to prove something. It was immaturity meeting immaturity in the worst way. In those moments, it didn't take much: just eye contact, a word taken the wrong way, or a stare held too long.

We claimed streets we didn't own, and repped gangs that tore our culture apart. Fighting over blocks that didn't belong to us.

Protecting pride that built nothing. We confused loyalty with destruction and mistook identity for territory.

After I finally broke free, someone pressed the cold barrel of a pistol against the back of my head, and I froze. Then it clicked.

Then it clicked again. And again.

My body went straight into shock.

When the person pulled the gun away to figure out why it was jamming, I snapped back into my body. I didn't think; I didn't look back. I just ran.

At the time, I didn't fully understand what had happened. I only knew I was still breathing. It wasn't until years later that I could see that moment with clarity. That's when I realized something bigger was at work. God's hand was over my life even when I didn't recognize it, even when I didn't value it.

Looking back, I understand that day differently. It wasn't just about surviving. It was a wake-up call. A reminder that my life still had purpose, even while I lived recklessly. What should have ended me instead interrupted me. It reminded me that grace is real. Protection is real. And sometimes mercy shows up in moments you don't deserve.

That moment didn't change me overnight. It didn't make me perfect. But it planted a truth in my spirit that never left me. I was still alive for a reason.

Moments like that force you to pause. They make you question why you're still breathing, what your life actually means, and what purpose might still await you if you're willing to step into it.

Reflection Questions

- Have you ever had a close call or wake-up moment, something that should have ended worse than it did?

....

....

....

....

....

- What do you think that moment was trying to tell you?

....

....

....

....

....

- If your life is still here for a reason, what responsibility comes with that truth?

....

....

....

....

....

Something as traumatizing as a near-death experience can really change a person's view on life. It certainly changed mine. I went from feeling invincible to understanding what a gift I had in life. I learned not to take my life for granted, though that took time.

By junior year, Mount Rainier had had enough of me, Turt, and Worm. They kicked us out and sent us to New Start in White

Center, an alternative school. A new chance. A new environment. Another opportunity to get it right.

I tried to be an academic. I tried to straighten up; I really did. But let's be real: when dysfunction and pain are all you've ever been fed, it's hard to digest anything healthy without choking on it.

Two months before graduation, I was kicked out again. I also learned I was going to be a father for the first time at almost eighteen years old. My mom was devastated.

And that was the moment I fully surrendered to the streets. I was lost. Lost and afraid. And when you're that lost, becoming a monster feels like control.

It was easy to become what I saw. That's all I knew. Whatever good that hung on by a thread? I cut it myself.

I became more money-motivated and game-oriented; I started touching money that felt real to me. Murda Block slangin' crack rocks. Out-of-state plug connections. Selling 8-balls, quarters, halves, zips. Wash, rinse, repeat.

Wayne, Jeezy, Twista, Kanye, Jay-Z, T.I., Juelz Santana, Gucci, Rose, and Plies; the music fed the image. I carried .40 cals, sawed-offs, and .22s while riding bubble Caprices, '87 Cutlasses, Cadillacs, and Dodge Magnums.

Eventually, I leaned harder into promoting prostitution. I told myself the risk was lower than selling dope. One day I had to hang onto a dope friend's car while it sped toward the freeway at forty miles per hour. I had to jump off to survive. That's when I realized the risk was higher than the reward.

But I didn't stop. I just changed lanes. I was a salesman either way. My mouthpiece was sharp. My personality was charming. From sixteen to twenty-one, people knew me as Papa the Pimp. Big Papa with the purple 'lac. Then pink and purple. Then cotton candy. Same Cadillac. Different paint jobs.

I made noise in that world. Even knocked a Cali pimp for his prostitute. If that sounds adventurous to you, let me correct that. It only got darker. I created more trauma, not just for others, but for myself. The feds built a case. People close to me got robbed, killed, or sentenced. People wanted to rob me.

More near-death moments occurred, like the one on Kent-Des Moines. Somebody jumped out of the bushes and shot at me point-blank while I was with my partner. Somehow I didn't even get grazed by a bullet. I don't have an explanation for why I've never gotten shot or sentenced long term. I thought I was untouchable, but it was nothing short of God's grace.

As I matured and ran into more life-altering trouble, that's when I started developing a shift in my mindset. Most of the friends I grew up with are dead or in prison. Living through that kind of reality forced me to recognize the need for genuine change, not just survival, but discipline.

The crucible of my near-death experiences is where my mindset shift was born. It became a set of principles and disciplines shaped by adversity, but crafted for success beyond it. At some point, I had to face a hard truth. Survival had kept me alive, but it could not build a future. Chaos had carried me for years, but it could not carry me any further. I needed order. I needed structure. And I needed to choose responsibility over impulse. That shift did not happen overnight. It happened through painful realizations, lost friends, quiet moments of reflection, and the understanding that staying reckless would only lead me to places I had already escaped from.

My mindset shift became my answer to that turning point. It was about being disciplined enough not to reverse the blessing of survival. It was about refusing to waste the second chance that life, and God, allowed me to have. And it was about learning how to live once I realized I had been spared, and respecting that survival comes with an assignment, not just relief. It was a defining shift for me. It was the moment when life stopped being about just staying alive and started being about living with intention, discipline, and accountability.

This mindset is a philosophy of my life rooted in self-control, focus, and a relentless pursuit of personal growth. It represents the moment my survival turned into purpose, and purpose turned into responsibility. It taught me that making it out is not the finish line. Staying out, growing forward, and building something meaningful is the real work.

First, I had to pay attention to the signs. God gives warnings before consequences. I ignored them for years. The arrests, the funerals, and the prison sentences surrounding me. Those weren't random. They were previews. Then I had to be honest with myself. If the people I associated with daily faced prison or death, it was only a matter of time before I stood in that same line.

Next, I had to cling to positive influences.

My mom and some of my siblings chose a better path. Instead of distancing myself, I drew closer. I needed spiritual guidance and real growth. I also had to become open to hearing uncomfortable truths. One day, a complete stranger, an older white man who looked like he needed help himself, flagged me down and spoke life into me while knowing nothing about me. His words hit. That moment shook me. Then came the hardest part: saying no. No to people. No to environments. And no to the version of myself addicted to chaos.

After that, I went dark and focused on deep heart work. Soul searching. It felt like rehab without a building. Surgery without anesthesia. Crying, praying, failing, getting back up, and repeating. I reached a point where I wanted to be good, not just for me, but for the people I would one day be responsible for. My future wife. My three daughters. My son. My legacy. That's when discipline stopped being optional. That's when faith stopped being decorative. And that's when resilience became daily work.

I've been to jail over ten times. Never longer than three days apiece. And that wasn't skill. That was mercy.

Some of you reading this are in the middle of that identity war. You're building a character because the real you feels too vulnerable.

Hear me clearly: it is never too late to change lanes. I thought I was solidifying who I was. But what I was really doing was stacking consequences. And eventually, consequences collect.

This is where this chapter ends, but the ride isn't over yet.

Because everything after this?

The consequences. The losses. The lessons. The growth. That's another journey entirely.

Reflection Questions

- What area of your life needs discipline, not excuses?

....

....

....

....

....

- What blessing do you risk losing if you continue living the same way?

....
....
....
....
....

- What does "growing forward" look like for you right now?

....
....
....
....
....

Loyalty to the Wrong Circle

This video dives deeper into what it means to be loyal to the wrong circle, and how your environment can either elevate you or eliminate you.

Closing Reflection: The Invitation

So, if failure was a person, and they knocked on your door tonight, would you let them in? Would you sit with them, even if it were uncomfortable? Would you ask them what they came to teach you?

Because the truth is, failure doesn't come to stay. It only visits long enough to hand you the keys to your next chapter.

Every setback is a setup for a comeback. Every closed door is a redirection, not a rejection.

NO means Next Opportunity. It is not the end. It is actually the opposite.

The next time failure visits, don't curse it.

Thank it. Learn from it. Then get up because your story isn't done yet.

Message to the Youth

I ain't here to preach to you. I'm here to remind you that I've been that kid who didn't believe tomorrow would look any different from today.

I've been the one with the *F* on the paper, with the weight on my shoulders, and the world saying, "You won't make it." But let me tell you something. They were wrong.

And if they were wrong about me, they might just be wrong about you too.

You might be sitting in a classroom, a group home, a cell, or maybe just stuck in your own head wondering when life's gonna give you a break.

But the truth is, life doesn't hand out breaks. It hands out lessons. And the same pressure trying to break you is actually shaping you.

Failure ain't the enemy, bro. It's the coach you don't like, but need the most. Failure's gonna pull up, talk crazy to you, and make you uncomfortable. That's how it teaches you. It'll check your pride, expose your fake friends, and strip away what's not real. But when the dust settles, what's left is you. Stronger. Smarter. Still standing.

So here's the deal.

Don't run from the pain. Learn from it.

Don't hate the process. Respect it.

And whatever you do, don't quit. Because quitting is the only thing that turns a lesson into a loss.

You ain't too far gone.

You ain't broken.

You're becoming.

And one day, somebody's gonna look at you and say, "Yo, if they made it out, I can too." So stand up. Brush off the dirt. And remember this.

You were never built to be perfect. You were built to bounce back.

— Anthony Curtis

Failure Is Only Permanent When You Quit

In this video, I break down why failure only becomes permanent when you stop trying, and how persistence is the real flex.

A Letter to My Younger Self

This letter is personal. It's the words I wish someone had spoken over me when I was younger. Read it slowly.

Acknowledgments

Immense love and gratitude to my wife, my peace, my reflection, and my anchor. And to my children, who remind me every day that love is a legacy. You are the reason I keep going, my heartbeat behind every word, and the proof that failure never wins when family is your foundation.

To my mother, who carried strength in silence and showed me how to keep pushing even when life was heavy, your fight built my faith.

To my father, whose lessons came through pain but planted the seeds of purpose.

To my brothers and sisters, we survived storms most people couldn't imagine. You are living proof that resilience runs in our blood.

To my grandma, Georgia Dean, the real MVP. You taught me that "Nothing beats a failure but a try." You squeezed me tight and whispered, "Don't let the Devil get you." Thank you for scaring the hell out of me, Grandma, because that fear turned into faith, and that faith carried me through. Your love, your prayers, and your lessons live throughout these pages.

To the friends I lost along the way, and the ones still fighting to find their way, this is for you too.

And finally, to Failure, the most misunderstood teacher I ever had. You didn't come to destroy me. You came to define me. Thank you for the lessons, the bruises, and the blueprint.

Special Thanks

To everyone who believed in me before the world caught up: the mentors, the partners, the homies, and the youth who remind me why I keep showing up.

To Chicago, for teaching me grit, survival, and the importance of keeping your head up even when your back's against the wall.

To Seattle, for giving me the space to rebuild, grow, and rise again.

To the teachers who saw more in me than my grades ever showed.

To the organizations, community partners, and people who gave me a shot when I didn't have one.

And to every young person out there still trying to figure it out, may this book be a mirror that reminds you of this truth: you are more than what you've been through.

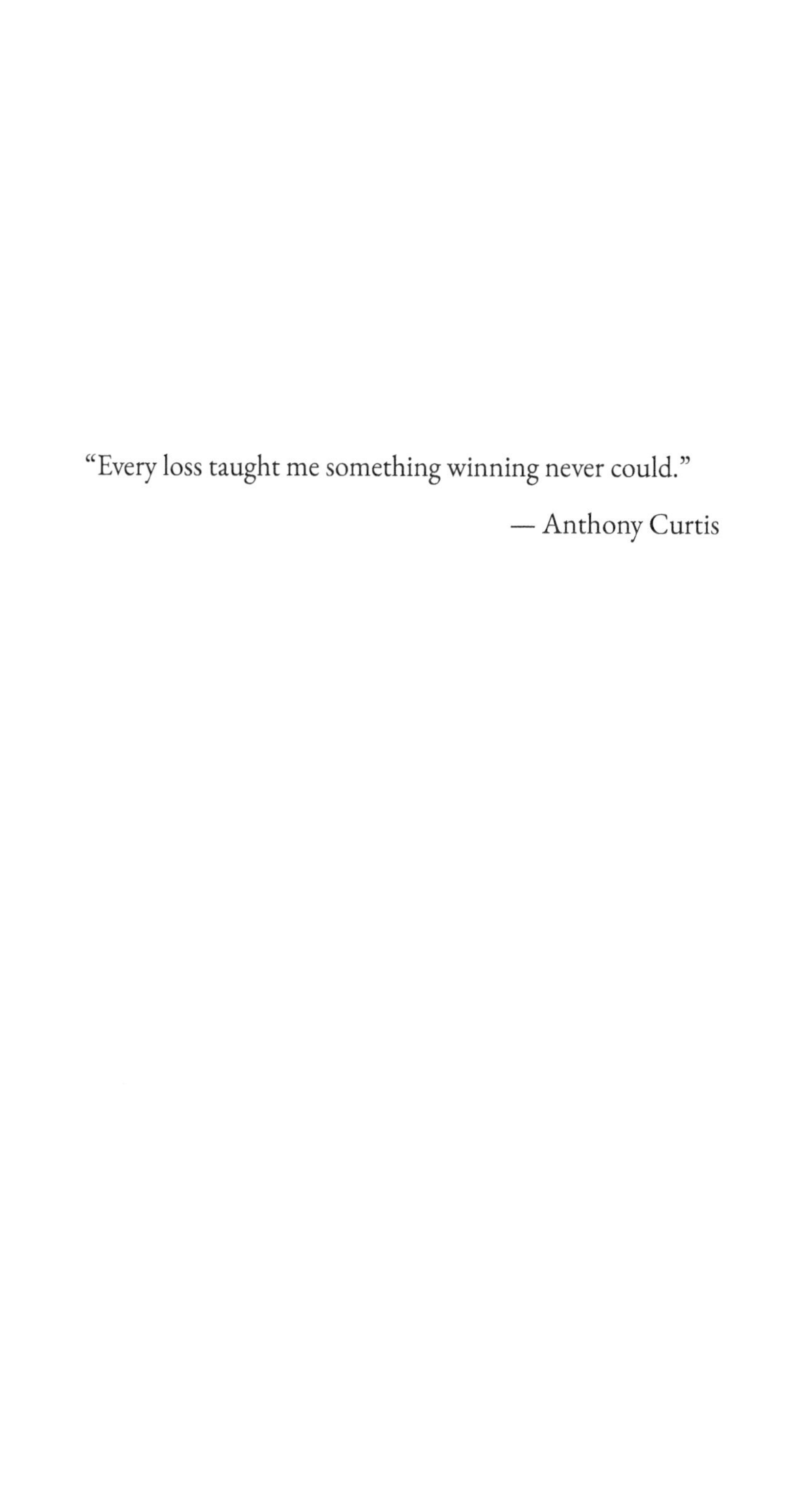

"Every loss taught me something winning never could."

— Anthony Curtis

About the Author

Anthony Curtis is a husband, father, youth advocate, speaker, and community builder from Chicago, Illinois, now rooted in the Pacific Northwest. As the founder and executive director of the Black Equality Coalition, Anthony has dedicated his life to empowering youth and families through mentorship, storytelling, and authentic relationship-building that meets people where they are.

His path, from surviving the streets of Chicago to building community power in Seattle, is one of redemption, resilience, and purpose. Anthony's voice reaches classrooms, detention centers, churches, and community spaces where young people see themselves reflected in his journey. His leadership continues to inspire others to rise above their circumstances and turn pain into purpose.

With *If Failure Was a Person*, Anthony continues his mission to redefine what success looks like, showing the next generation that the *F* on your paper doesn't mean FAIL, it means First Attempt in Learning.

"I didn't write this book to talk at you. I wrote it to talk with you, because I've been you."

www.ingramcontent.com/pod-product-compliance
Lightning Source LLC
LaVergne TN
LVHW010545100826
845148LV00013B/2613

* 9 7 9 8 2 3 4 0 5 1 0 1 1 *